Monotone World Celebrations
Collected Poems
by Steven Amash

Thank you for the support!
So great to know you!

"Forsythia" and "Words to Myself in Silence, the Most Addicting Drug" were previously published by Punchnel's in October of 2014.

For Wendy

Monotone World Celebrations

October Passing-

Strange what happens in October
That subtle way the world changes
That sharp contrast of colors on the sky
That unimaginable zest for something
        that is new

Strange that I think of October
And not of the way that you have
        moved on

That I think of the way the
        leaves have turned
                but you never come up

Though you are there, I'm sure
        tucked against the
small things that I have put off

Your smile and your crooked nose
        and gasps of ecstasy and
longing for more

They are there, I'm sure,
        but today I've seen the sky
and can no longer look down

Strange what a season can do
and what new love can never
        take away from life

Strange the inconsistencies that
keep consistent
        the passing of time

On Working Overtime-

When each entry is a note
on how we arrive home late
and wake again early,
there is no hope
in the present and no
sleep for repair

But the two of us are dealing with
this in our own ways:

I in my solitude and you in
your solitude; the two unrelated but
for the words

I know this morning
could have been different
for us, but now cannot

And the moment is gone

And it causes the pain that
causes the pain that
causes the pain to cause
the rehearsal of conversations
within the gates of our mind

It's one mind, no longer
flattering to speak about

Still, we must remember the
ways in which we handle our
situations and the situations of
the spouses, whom we assume
are less fortunate than us

And people come and people
go on their way

Before we know it, this
moment, too, is gone

Moon Thoughts-

Here where the sun goes to die,
you and I, myself and the imagination,
recline among the stones and weeds
and sand between stitches of thread

Your hands feel my hands,
though no fingers touch

Tonight no fingers touch

Here you say the moon is in orbit
and that it watches us each night
until a time when it consumes us
and we are left in the sky
to orbit around our lives

We look down on what we hold close

You say this is the orbit of life:
so we are watched,
so we watch in the end

What bones lie beneath us,
miles below the sand and stone?

What hourly wages are beneath
the dust at our feet?

Nothing, nothing but the moon
can orbit without the restraint of time

We are mere shadows of the waning
in the time that the moon draws our cycles,
counts our promises, and houses nothing
of our shortcomings and successes

You tonight, my angel, define the shadows
in the face of the moon

The First Conversation-

I found you there,
so much a reflection
of all I've ever lost
and all that I was yet
to discover

It was all waiting there within you
and within your bourbon smile
and your monochrome eyes,
your familiar voice that spoke
to me between my presumptive thoughts
of the woman I saw before my broken body,
no longer open to change

With your words it was winter and
with your blessing I had summer in my mind
and that's where I found you and found
in you myself
and myself seeking embrace, closure, insecure
beginnings and, above all,
hope

Stream of Consciousness-

I can't remember the words that rambled from my mouth as I lay on the couch, one leg on the ground, passing into unconscious thought. Like the rain passing over my roof, so are the words of drunken stupor washed into the gutter outside my apartment.

The idea that stream of consciousness pasted together pictures on the bar room wall was brought up in conversation with another girl that I left sitting at the table last night. Pictures of trees and hallways leading to doors and staircases, all juxtaposed to a large picture of a beautiful girl with a placid smile on her lips. Gazing at me from behind the chair where another friend sat talking to a young woman with dark hair flowing down her shoulders, the picture haunted me. For a moment I wanted to love her. For a moment I may have loved her.

And so the night went on with me falling in and out of love with a picture pasted on a wall behind two beautiful women who would never match the beauty that I've seen in the eyes of tranquility hanging before me.

If the picture had fallen from the wall, my imagination would have led me to believe she could have been pasted again upside down so as to know her from another angle. But again, the picture tangled my emotions, and walking home I thought of nothing but anger and resentment to those that have defiled the beautiful ones, who are few.

Jaded are the youthful. Jaded are those with keen eyes. Jaded are those who once knew love. Jaded are the long haired flower children who are no more. Jaded is the photograph of a girl, captured, immortalized on a bar room wall before the world could get her, and men rip apart the soul's placenta. Jaded am I, laying on blankets, running my mouth to the cushions.

She got away, the girl in the photograph. I didn't take her home. I took nothing home, but left there in the bar room a stream of consciousness, waiting and reaching for a girl I thought I loved, if only for a moment.

Little Italy-

Coffee cup lids,
biodegradable,
stacked in rows
by gorgeous girl–
perfect–
pouring sugar
in glass jar

slightly cold
customers
keeping quiet
the sad cafe

accordion sounds
in Little Italy
music

gorgeous,
she would be,
dancing in the street
but for winter

Leave Me Bare-

Dance with me, sweet summer wind
Lay your hand upon my chest
Feel the empty sigh of sorrow
In every moment and in each breath
I sing to you, leave me bare

By the river's silent shore
I reach into every outward gaze
Piercing into every heart, my love
Whispering welcome home to me
Sing for me, the gentle breeze

Men are taught to love the wind
Like the fountains endless flow
Sweet breaths whisper in the mist
And chase until we lose ourselves
I sing to you, leave me bare

There is a street that we once knew
In between the falling leaves
Where rain has washed the road away
To leave us wandering in the sand
By the river's silent shore

Come along one more time
To the depths that we have known
And climb with me into the shade
Of barren trees and desert roads
One last time, I sing to you

Dance with me into the fall
Of touch and taste of better times
Breathe the empty sigh for me
In everything, I wait for you

Pale Fading-

The pale fading of each sunset
is an image of new birth
in the heavens,
merely a death upon the earth.

And at the end of each day,
as I take that walk down from the field
and up my quiet driveway in town,
I question why loneliness comes at sunset.

Is it that each sunset is a subtraction of a
loved one;
a brother, a sister, or a co-worker?

Is it that each sunset is the first person to
leave the party and the first realization
that everyone will eventually leave?

Is it death that is so sad, or the understanding
that we must persist, fearing
the inevitable fate, progressively alone
as the ones we love split the curtain of the void?

As I reach my door, and darkness comes,
there is a light from the hall and a footstep's
hollow echo on the stairs, and my love
telling me that it's getting late.

What is left for the man with everything,
but to count each sunset and record each
drop of rain, each fallen angel and
each star, free falling in the night?

Like a Tree-

Like a tree, I have stood before the wind
I am torn from my roots and battered in the breeze
I lie drifting through the sea and am washed ashore
To the beach my sisters ran upon as children
My branches are snapped, my life is waterlogged
And weighed down by the salt of the earth

When I Say That I Love You-

When I say that I love you
I say truthfully that I adore the memory
Of a girl I met in the starlit banks of an autumn night
Blue eyes beneath a pale complexion
Where we treated the night to the dance of the morning

When I say that I love you
I say truthfully that I adore the memory
Of a night comprised of gestures to leave the longing
Petite beauty in my own embrace
The night we forgot what it meant to be lovers

When I say that I love you
I say truthfully that I adore the memory
Of the shadow of a girl on a park bench
Golden hair of a Sunday morning
When we dressed in white before a new family of hope

When I say that I love you
I say truthfully that I adore the memory
Of the moment when life was brought to my lungs
Safety that I've sought since birth
On the morning I was loved forever in a moment

My Woman, I Guide You to the Window-

My woman, I guide you to the window
I write the same three words on your palm
I lay down beside you in the moonlight
And I run into the comfort of your holy arms

Where I lay and contemplate the science
Of how man and woman are brought
To believe in the miracle of lovers
And taught to leave the ones who are not

But I'll never be turned in hatred
Toward the ones who can't understand truth
And toward the men who have grown out of loving
To grasp at the flowers of youth

And the ones that dance before the mirror of beauty
With one hand on their lifeless thigh
In a room where darkness is forgotten
And the roses from your honeymoon still lie

Beside the switchblade and the brandy
On the rug that you knelt once before
Where you loosened the buckles of boredom
And lay yourself out on the floor

But the time has come for the morning
And the thoughts of the past have been maimed
Like the lilies I cut from your gardens
And the snow covered ones that remain

And from the window I can see the fruit trees
Where I stood in the rain when you left
And the gutter where I felt each droplet
With the mist on the day we first met

Where a blanket of leaves coat the doorway
Of a house that I thought I once knew

Where the children all play in silence
With their very first glances of you

I could draw you into the memory
Of myself outside on the lawn
Like a painter with one last sunbeam
Lighting the grass that we once walked upon

But the window is open at our fingers
And the swaying of the blade has begun
Where upon I swing in the silence
As I gently reach to pull you on

Our beauty, cries the pane of the window
And our wretchedness calls the chill of the frost
But the love from my mind never whispers
Not after all of ourselves we have lost

From a Cross-

My love, I hang from each word you throw me
Like Christ on the cross
I hang from each word
I reach for each reason
And know there are none
I crawl to you like a rat
On the cold embankment of an icy glen

Come to me, come to me
I am calling, "Come to me!"
No one is listening
All around me is laughter

My love, you've broken me together
And have taken me down
Like Christ
To the world
My woman, my woman!
Why have you forsaken me?

Prologue to Myself at the Moment-

I am the blinded child
I am the blinded woman, redeeming herself from herself
I am the teacher, struggling to get the point across on this paper
I am the mother at home, staring at the television
I am the man at the cafe, reading the New York Times
I am the short list of women that I've written on my heart
I am the whore of Vienna
I am the angel on your bed post
I am the flower on your lampshade
I am the man outside your window, waiting for the light to turn on
I am the street corner pauper
I am Conrad's search for darkness
I am the wilderness child that I used to be
I am the dark eyed girl behind the counter in another loveless town
I am the love that I gave to you
I am the fingerprints on the telephone
I am the coffee grounds in my brother's eyelashes
I am Young Scott, who never came home from war
I am the Polish waitress, married to an American
I am the idea of plastic ivy flower pots
I am the eighteen wheels on Nebraska plains
I am the tailor
I am Paul Simon's face and hands
I am the medicine for grief
I am the death of my grandmother
I am the blue eyes in everything I do
I am the forsaken sons and daughters of "God Bless America"
I am the "Lord have mercy on us all"
I am the only "Hallelujah" that I couldn't believe
I am the young boy with the beautiful eyes on a train ride home
I am the fur around your neck
I am the love affair that ended your lies
I am the turnpike to my sister's womb

I am the book in my closet
I am the pine needle on my staircase
I am the door frame to your bedroom that you locked yourself into
I am the sex that you dreamt of last night
My brother, I am your untrimmed hair
I am your lover from high school
I am your overplayed record of sorrow
I am the long summer car ride through the valley
I am the children, parading in unison
I am Gershwin's "I love you"
I am the five faces of my democracy
I am the make up on my beautiful barista
I am the blue eyed oracle of Great Barrington
I am the bitter taste of a morning in December
I am the stare of your eyes into mine
I am the song I sang to an empty room
I am the need to resist companionship
Oh, I am the teenager in love
I am the empty hole in everybody's longing
I am the lull in all the busy days we spent alone
My brother, I am the compromise to your inferno
I am the sorry side of the life that I couldn't save you from

Naked #2-

Back home to the rush
A corner TV screen
Rumbling war through the static
Like tension between the old man
And the children at bar room tables
On fog covered nights
Staring from the window
Into the white washed,
Halo lit, sidewalk cracks
Dreaming in bed
Of clouded surfaces
Skipping through town naked
To the beat of a steady 3/4
On the music man's tambourine
Footed bass drum pedal
Singing like a siren to Caspian
At the helm of the morning
Where I wake to the clouds
And rain drying asphalt puddles
Wishing it were all a dream

On Waiting-

In the art
Of waiting
There is a period
Where all the pain
Swells and then dissolves
Into the hole
Of our longing mind
After this
There is nothing

Locks-

The body is bloated
And setting the scene
For another night alone
In the intersections of
My dark bedroom
That I locked you from

I locked you from many things
I locked you from many days, my love

I locked you from
The mirrors in my eyes
Now we are only reflections
Of one another
In the horrible expanse
That we have called love
There is no word for this pain

-----------First Notepad-------------

#1 Driver Seat Window-

I think about it
As I step from my car
Gazing into the window reflection
Seeing another man
Pointing for me to go back
I see the brown hairs individually fall
From my head to the freckles
That grace my baby's face
Christina, you've left a ribbon
Unwound in my mind
Like the hubcap spinning off of
The lemon law dream that you sold me
Still painted in my eyes with the reflection
Of another man in my driver's seat
It's been a long drive from yesterday
Already gazing into the past of tomorrow

#2 Love Note (If I Were a Chord, I'd Be E Minor)

I've changed my mind
So many times
Each day I wake
To find
You gone and running
Scared from my life
That I've given
You
And maybe it is
Too soon
To choose a life
That we must
Win and lose
Equal amounts of
Ourselves daily
To satisfy the
Marriage bed
Maybe I've lied
About being happy
And now I long
For you
Like you long
Against me

#3 I Am Charles Bukowski-

The counter's clean for once
And she doesn't call me
Because she has another man
Touring her through the hills above Sausalito
Into late night camp trips
And early Sunday morning hikes down California
While I'm here touching myself
And reading Bukowski
Wondering what the big deal is
I too have been hungover three days straight
Yet have been sober for months
Listening to the cat on the fire escape
Clawing at the window above my kitchen
As a threesome takes place
Somewhere on the top floor
Leaving the bathroom faucet running down the drain
I'm questioning why my neighbors
The sole reason for breaking my concentration
Wear led boots and iron slippers
I'm left questioning why I can love you
And feel nothing in return
But pain and drunken thinking
Bukowski had it all wrong
The cat must be taking a dip in the tub
As the stairwells are filled with iron toe echoes
And I am left writing notes
At the clean counter

#4 Phone Call Regrets-

During the phone call
There were things
Not mentioned from my end
The first being the inevitable weight
Of another season's extinction
Leaving me to feel rushed
The second being the nausea
Passed in each synapse
As I go about my daily life
That you've joyfully pranced from
And the third being the love
That neither of us feels
For each other
Anymore

#5 Caverns-

I feel better
When the day's done
And I shut out the lights
And lock myself in the bathroom
Under the warmth of the shower head
Washing away dirt and distrust
And clouded images
That make up my night time endeavors
Into moonlit caverns
That I've exploited to young women
In grocery stores and cafes
All around the north east
Receiving in return
Brilliant and radiant smiles
That I store in jars
By my bedside where I lay
Drifting between you and her

#6 First Impressions-

Monday night and I've forgotten
To tell her something about myself
Anything would have done
But she leaves with a first impression
Much like mine of her
Maybe it won't work out tonight
Instead of telephoning again
I just lay in my boxers
And drink a half gallon of water
From a carcinogenic bottle I bought
Before cancer was big
I sit up itching my back
Like I've got the plague
Under my skin
Where I used to have you

#7 In Hostel Pinning-

There are no stars tonight
I'm inside and the ceiling
Is off white with spider webs
Strewn over my bed sheets
And draped over the pictures
I've pasted of you
Somewhere in my memory waiting
For a thumb tack to pin you
To the wall
As I did at the Post and Taylor crossroads
Giving you the chance to imprint
Yourself on me as you would
Knowing someday I'd take note
And while alone, read to you
Watching you take yourself home
For the last time passing through my door

#8 Cheap Cabernet Flowers-

For weeks now I've stared
Into the dark bottles, half full
With water for the dead flowers
Poking out of each cheap cabernet
And creating homes for the wildlife
That creep through the cracks
In the window screens that I keep closed
For fear of somebody's insight
And expectations of you
As if I fear the wax dripping
From the candles on the TV, book shelves, desk tops,
Dressers, window sills, et cetera
Creating a mystic appearance in our embrace
Waltzing with the bitter rose between my teeth
Withered like the wedding dress
Over my shoulder being stored in the closet

#9 Made in Hollywood-

We used to talk humanely
When we looked at pictures and stills
Of Scarlett O'Hara and the dresses
She wore in the longest love story
We'd ever seen together
She doesn't let me think of her now
We have a keen eye on today
And tomorrow, but no further than that
And I pick her up
And we drive off together
Making love all night
Before I drive her back home
Waking up to do it all over
The next day
Until one day she's not there to pick up
Yet I'm still glad that like love
She knows Scarlett O'Hara was made in Hollywood

#10 Worthless Son-

I'll give it one last try
I say to myself
Head under pillow, eyes wide open
For three days unable to sleep
Night times filled in dreamland mutterings
Give me a break, sand man
I'm twenty some odd years dead
And groaning with alcohol know how
In my veins like a happy hour junky
After being sober for who knows how long
If I wasn't chained to this bed
By the world and you and me
I'd be making something of my life
Even in the wee hours that I cry
From sleep deprivation
I'd be making something of my life

#11 Crosby's Puddle-

It's going on eleven o' clock tonight
And I'm splashing ankle deep
In insomniac thunder storm escapades
Suddenly waking up to find that I did
Indeed fall asleep last night
Somehow surviving for another day
Taking my clothes from the rack
And bracing myself before going back to bed
Waking up ten minutes later
To the sound of the alarm clock
And the alarm clock at the other side
Of my narrow little cubicle
I'm at work suddenly
Shy of any feelings for the faces
The hard faces that watch me
Trying to drown quickly
In ankle deep puddles

San Francisco-

San Francisco,
Where the faces of the street
Are the faces of dogs
Like the woman, running from the night
Her face like an animal
Starved
Sprinting down Market Street

San Francisco,
Where the homeless men
Look like the Oakland homeless men
Who look like the New York homeless men
Who all look like the homeless man I met
In Bennington when I was just seventeen
And naive enough to give the man a dollar

Where the children rush beside
The parents, waiting for a fix from the candy store
Holding out each hand and always
Getting what they need

Where I saw the same man each night
Playing on the Wharf
to a violin with no strings

Where the morning wakes new faces
In blankets under the bare trees
Waiting for night fall
To let them dream

Where the romance is forgotten
To a ship wreck off the coast
Of a forsaken island

Watching the boats of the chosen
Ascending like pilgrims to understand
the country's means of power

Where still beneath the waves
Countless others wait to surface
To the heights of the redwoods
That we sat beside in pictures
"Click"
Will you remember me tomorrow?

San Francisco,
At the cafe on Kearny
Thinking of home and a dusty guitar
By the bedpost
And returning only to find myself
Shuffling down the streets and alleys
Looking for you in a dream

I don't mention now the nights
Spent alone in bed with the silence
Of an alarm clock that won't keep time
Or the empty tears that fall
On the black pillow case
Where your hair still lies illuminated
Hanging on as if to say
"Don't forget me just yet"

San Francisco,
With it's cry across the bay
To a city I once loved in the rain
Seeping through the cracks in a street corner
Holding an umbrella above your head like a halo

San Francisco, have you forgotten?
Have you forgotten the face of a beautiful boy
In the city cellar
Reminding me of the friend I once knew as a child?

San Francisco,
Your face follows me home at night
I see your face in the reflection of the clothing stores
And dark cafes

But at night I see darkness
At night I hear silence
But even the silence gives way
To the rain, dripping down my window tonight

City on the Water-

So much has been written about you
Great city on the water
The world shone it's light on your windows
And you remained quiet in your temple
Your eyes were battered with dust
From the world around you crumbling
But you stood strong at the entrance to Canaan
I walked long for you, holy light shedder
Do not turn your face from me
And close your iron doors to your son
Have not the lessons of your brothers
Taught you nothing of your world
Sweet city on the water

From a Hill in Oakland-

From atop the hill
I saw the face of my father
Etched in the clouds
Looking upon me and the water in the bay
And the water in the quarry
Behind the empty insurance agency
That now acts as a home to rosemary hedges
And barren plum trees
I saw my father
Etched in the sky
Dedicating his face to the blue above America
Where he will never know the truth of the land
Where he will never touch the gold of the fields
And never feel the warmth of the pavement
Running hard below my feet
On the clear autumn morning
You are safe in your sky, father
And I am safe in my hedges
Above the hill, going skyward
And to the ocean that you loved as a child

Leaving California-

Oh, blue sky turning yellow along the frames
With the sunset over San Francisco coming to it's climax,
Bright and beautiful, yet dim enough to stare into for hours,
Or minutes, or that short bit of charity that's given to lovers at the end of the day
The water flows through the bay and hits the docks
Like a touch from that old friend I used to know,
Now lost out east to the mediocrity of everything that used to exist for me.
When the sun goes down over the west coast,
It's realized how long it takes to once again rise
The man at the end of the dock can take his pictures all evening
And I can sit here scribbling illegible notes to all the women I love,
But I'll never be able to lift that sun over this sad world
And it is a sad world as I watch the last lovers separate themselves
To the coming darkness, and the couple on basket-ed bikes
Commenting on the beauty of the sky, which isn't beauty at all
But still will make for a nice memory at some point
And they're not even touching as they lean against the guard rail,
Simply feeling the cool west coast air falling around them
And the trains are coming to rest at the station of Jack London
As I'm waiting on mine and getting up to walk at the side of the water
Thinking of Mom, Dad, lover, brother, sisters and all my own stupidity
And the distance between tonight and tomorrow,
And on the dock I simply sigh a goodnight to myself
And close my eyes to San Francisco on the horizon for the last time.

Jack London Square
Oakland, CA
Sunset 9/30/12

Father-

Father, I have seen the face of the world
I have seen the mad man dance in the forest
And the blind man crawl the avenue
In the darkness I saw the light of a thousand eyes
pointing to an unbelievable god in the sky
And to him I called your name

I sat in my room and wrote a letter to the wind
asking for the forgiveness of you, Father
And the letter was rejected for incorrect
use of the word Poetry
The picture of the poet haunts me
And watches every pen scratch that I make
You, Allen, are painted on canvas
And dripping to the puddle at my feet

The ribbon of questions lays long in the river
and threads it's needle through my toes
that sink in silence with the sand on the shore

Oh, sweet father in your prison
Are the faces of your children
illuminating your madness
and guiding you to the shores of this river
where I sit waiting for you?

My heart cries for you more today
than for any woman I have loved
Father, your face lights the darkness
When will this ribbon be unwound
and set free to be strung in the night?
The coat tails of your past are fading
as you dance further toward the river

I wake to a cry in the darkness of my home
And feel the tears of my mother beside me in the bed
Where the pillow remains wet
And where out the window a man paints
the snow of childhood to the mountains

Waking Up Again (Just Asleep)-

And I'm half asleep
Moon hidden under curtain
Light bulb burning windowed eyes
And roommate in loveless romance
Outside door with petite woman
It's all over now, baby cakes
The night is like a bedpost
Gripping me and holding tight
So as to not let me drop on tomorrow
Before getting a good time alone
Reaching for the ceiling organs
Stretching higher and higher
Each time I let one off
Like fireworks bursting into
Monotone world celebrations
Black and white, maybe a bit milky
Lasting until running eggs fill the pan
In early morning when I run out quick
Catching the last breath of exhaust
As the car whimpers into itself
And fades away from the road
Parked on the gravel
Holding firm a spot near the apartment
Fool I am here running myself to sleep
Making the midnight blues
Counting my fingers and toes
For morning and the sunrise or sunset
Of another day or night or afternoon fading
Here we go again into oblivion
That blueberry bowl's on the ground
Saying farewell, goodnight sweetheart
And will be there in the morning
Purple like a lilac in heat festered city summer
Making love to the dew in the humidity
Of young romance and sex and saliva
Passed between two hopeful youths
There's not a knock tonight from the room next door

It's sleep and coffee in few hours after the fact
And I'm at work in those moments
As the neighbor weighs the breakfast
Toast and eggs and pills and smoke
Or it's a drive into town
Hearing that old engine running slow
Like a beat dog cowering in the open
With the young men doing the cobblestone filth
As here I am lying through my teeth
In all those little bedtime stories
Read every night into your little eardrums
I'm a liar, your mommy, your satan, your angel
I've been lied to and that's okay
Go ahead give me a bedtime story
I tell the kid this from my own sad eyes
Watching him on the sidewalks of my busy street
Someplace in my head I'm feeling the safety of mommy's words
Thrown in somewhere between daddy's lies
Still unable to sleep with the blankets tied around my neck

Last Thoughts-

Let those who seek me
Be turned away in anger
When I waken to be unshaven
A man with no future of Messiah-like
Rides through the waters of Galilee
Let those who seek me
Be turned away in hatred and disgust
When they find my thin body
Shriveled and kissing the face
Of my killers, the loveless
Let those who seek me
Do so in the dry flowers
That I passed on to you

Above Town-

Sitting naked, alone again
At the brim of the darkness
That now seeps through town
Below my feet and dreaming
Through all the crooked stones and steps
That lead to the big wooden doors
Of the church that I see from the window
Of the bedroom at Park Street
The bells hit eleven for the hours
I've wasted here loveless
Like the rest of the drifters
Above this town, facing the night
And the flitter of the little wings in the dark
With the chatter and squeals of the bat
Speaking the unspoken language
In the same way we live our lie

Another Riverside Evening-

I come to the river at sundown
On Friday afternoons
When the air lives with mosquitos
And the night falls slowly on the water

The trees are painted yellow
By the sun on certain evenings
When I choose to watch the world
Through the eyes of a bird

In the moments when all stops moving
I can hear the trees alight with laughter
At the young man sitting riverside
Trying to capture another man's life

The Clearing-

Lover, I have taken you through the clearing
I have rinsed the face from your body
Your eyes no longer shine through me
Your hair no longer wraps around my mind
The glow of your silence no longer haunts me
Where now is your forever mindless skin?
You have torn away for yourself a dwelling
And I have stripped each wall of yours
Down to the last thumb tack and pin hole
I have loosed your blood from the bowels of man
And have tasted the waste at your fingers
I have lost you and left you for dead
You who come in lust, pride, no shape, and happy
I will watch your blood trickle
And I will let it

Portland Blues #1

I'm coming down
A new town
A new line of faces
A row of lights on a darkened street
The world is lit like magic

I'm coming down from the rooftops
I saw in a dream
A man above the city
Who watched with open eyes
The sea of sockets
Crawling on the sidewalk below

The sky gave nothing to me
When I stared into it's darkness
It's night and there is no sky

I'm coming down
And things begin to dim around me
The women around me turn ugly
And older than they were
All the fine dressed children surround me
With costumes of night

It is night
I am coming down
The love I felt is gone
The city I have whored myself to is gone
The books on my table are mere pornography
Even the woman at the counter is aging
The rain begins to fall
Jesus is calling his saints for Sunday
Saturday has summoned me again
To call the children from their houses

Portland Blues # 2

I'm drinking again
The rivers are raging
My body is waiting
The women in tight pants
Are leaving the doors
The river is parted
East and west are one

I'm touching the ambers of Pacifica
Didn't I know you once before?
A long spring afternoon
I tasted the salt from your fingers
And dipped into your pools
Beside the tall hills of York
We were another world then
We were smaller oceans
Touching a similar shore

Cancer when will I touch your embers?
When will I understand devotion?
When will the sun bathe my love for you?

I am drinking again of you
You have not asked for me
As I have not asked for tomorrow
I am coming down now

Does the rain stop in Portland?
Or does it fall to separate us
Sweet east side of life

I'm drinking again
And placing my fist on the counter
Calling for the doubtless to join me

Union Station in Rain-

There was a flash of light
As if the world were born
Above the highest building of Portland
Where I stood below
Gazing into the windows on the corner
Where there stood a line of men
Miscreants, Ne'r-do-wells, vagabonds, losers
The ones who had played a hand
Destined to recycle in failure without pity
The men were faceless through the glass
A sign would label this exhibit "old age"
And all would go on as life should

There was a light above Portland
As a helicopter sounded over the river
Passing behind the customs building
And then fading to the horizon
Leaving me to watch the day fall to the clouds
Soon the blue sky would be gone
And the rain would fall back into place
And all would go on as life should

There was a light inside a small taxi cab
That a man and woman climbed into
The man was handsome and the woman beautiful
But they were only two more people in the rain
Running beside the station like children
As I watched from the bench under the awning
Counting the sounds of the clock tower
Knowing that soon it would be night
and the stars would not shine over Portland
And all would go on as life should

A Small Apartment in Great Barrington-

She told me it scares her
The way I live alone in a small room
She said it makes her cry
And it does, I've been there before
I told her that I'm fine
I told her that I just might be crazy enough
To be a man for this life
This kind of life

She left me a few days later
I see her now every few months
Out of the corner of my eye
When she shops for lettuce
And small bottles of wine
That we never drank together
And it doesn't bother me anymore

When I walk back in the rain
And climb the stairs to my room
I find rose petals in the carpet
And leave them to dry tomorrow
In the sunlight through the window
That they told me just might come

When I shut the blinds
I shut my mind off of her
I know that the speakers still crackle
From the records in the closet
But they're her voice
And it's all I have until tomorrow
When the sun will come out

Words to Myself in Silence, the Most Addicting Drug-

It's Sunday afternoon in November
The phone is dead because I'm not speaking
I've sentenced myself to silence
And am now typing to you with lack of reason
Montana is cold and uninteresting
The snow falls down in various hours of night
The morning brings a lit cloud covering
And all the people walk the streets in black coats
Myself among them, mustached and sober
Green felt flat cap on head, drinking coffee
From a quiet little cafe down Central

How are the early morning Oakland clouds?
Do they still rise at noon over 38th and Broadway
Shining light on my memories of you?
Have you left your hair ties on his nightstand?
My poems remind me of our love affair
And of the words I put in your mouth

I'm watching a film of Paris
And now long to sleep with you in Corso's attic
Staring out the windows under the patron saint of lost causes
Watching the rain fall onto my fingertips at the windowsill

Imagine the train to Vienna where I danced with you in December
And kissed your hair with the vice at my jaw

There's a wood stove in the living room
And we keep it going from noon to dusk
The fire burns itself out when the door is left open

I bought my ticket to the bay a few days ago
And have decided to stay for fear of growing old

In the memory of a man scattering photographs face down on the floor
It's growing late and the hidden sun is setting

Will we talk before we meet again and ride the train to Berkeley?
Or will I catch the train to Vienna in the springtime
Holding the hand of Saint Jude as the rails wind their crooked path?

From an Old Montana Ranch-

There's a highway beside the cow pastures
Of the old ranch where I'm living
The cars rush by at seventy-five
And I can hear the trucks from my window
Some mornings I walk to the mailbox
And watch the old cars beat their path
I sometimes watch myself leap between the yellow
And get taken by tractor trailers in full gear
My body being dragged down highway 93
Most mornings I walk back to the cabin quietly
And sit beside the fire with the paper
Reading about yesterday and all that has happened
My face is yet to appear on the headlines for murder
And of this I am grateful to myself
When the afternoon comes I gather wood for the stove
And carry it in large apple boxes up the pine stairs
I watch the same broken-fisted crow fly the fields
And see each new sight all over again
When the night comes the stars light the great blackness
I stand off the porch with my coat around me
Gazing at the similarities between the worlds
In the morning I get the paper and die all over again

Insomnia Poem-

Things have changed
It's three AM and I'm awake
Under the living room light
With a cup of hot chocolate
And a fly that wants to murder itself
on the lightbulb
But can't seem to succeed

I was asleep by ten
I'm almost sure of it
I had two gin & tonics
and three ales in me
And felt tired enough
after walking home

I've been trying now
To get back to sleep
For three hours
And I think that I may be
giving up

I don't intend to take off
all my clothes
and attempt to sleep again
I keep thinking that maybe I'm tired
But I'm sure of it
I'm not

Do all the doubts of love and death
come in the hours
that we're supposed to be asleep?
I feel that we sleep
to hide ourselves from the fear
My company and I resort to darkness
when our lives blot out the sun

South Street in Snow-

Cold and sitting again
Singing a song for the typewriter
That sits alone on the windowsill
Overlooking the driveway where the cars are parked
In a row facing South street
That drops down to town
Freshly paved over summer
And now being covered by snow

The wind twists the ice in patterns
Around the spotlight by the door
And back home the railings are lit multicolored
A strand of lights hangs dark in the night
And a friend's present lays alone
Under a tree of ornaments
One by one dropping to the ground

Tonight the sky could fall over the world
And silence the air between the people
Who speak in ribbons of snow
Tonight the world may never know
That the sky has fallen

Beside the window I sit, cold
Painting pictures in my mind
And silently singing for the typewriter
Back home on the windowsill
Beside the bed
Where you lay in a dream
Of what you missed
While you were busy loving

Cafe on Sunday Morning-

The setting of Sunday cafe
Busy, bustle, big city folk
The hurry of small town folk
To clear the table
Serve the plates
And otherwise keep everything warm
Quiet small town in disarray
Where has your sabbath gone?

With coffee cup in hand
Stirring the useless piece of wood
Trying to scrape up the sugar
Settled on the bottom
I look at each face
Sitting this Sunday morning
With their own coffee cups
And their own useless stirrers
I can't recognize any of them
But, again, can't make out the face
Through the back of an old woman's head
And wonder if I know her
Maybe in a dream
She still sits facing the window
I only turn now and then
To see her gazing at the snow
That fell last night

A couple dressed in snow attire
With two fat and useless children
Come in and wonder where to sit
They have never been in a cafe before
And are in a hurry to eat
Though I worry that they will most likely
Not know how to do that
Despite their fat, useless children

A family with a baby sit behind me
And try to make it speak words

The waiter eggs them on
And the baby remains quiet
Too tired to really care
I guess that he will grow
To resent his stupid parents
And burn his millions in a campfire
While reclaiming some sort of life
That his parents never gave him

Three men who have known each other
For sometime now, come to eat
There is a table of five seats
And they claim three of them
Evenly dispersed, leaving two empty chairs
Where two wives would be sitting if they had married
But none have married
The third man is too young to know love
And he is the closest to marriage
of the three...
He has an orange beard
And looks to know nothing of women
But he knows enough to understand
That it is better that way
And he smiles to himself
And continues talking to his old friends

The young waiter shuffles by
Like a freight train
On his route to the bus bin
And looks at me and smiles
As the young lady fills my cup
And is glad that I smile back
She knows I always smile
When the coffee is reheated
And I still will only give tips
Of fifty cense at the counter

I have seen Aphrodite in an apron
Working above the ovens and cooling racks
In a small box with a window behind the counter
There is a door that swings to the kitchen
And each time it sways
I catch sight of her ankles

Under dark jeans
Engaged to the body above them
Just as they say she is engaged to the man
Who sits at the large table by the door
He's treated like royalty by the staff
And I would treat him like royalty too
But I've never known him
And choose rather to acknowledge his nonexistence
Than to admit all is hopeless

Goddess in the kitchen
Don't you see me here
Staring into your eyes?
My last sight on earth
And I would die happy
At this counter alone

Unexamined and undiscovered
Oh, were you my angel
Or my goddess?
Lonely, like all women are
I would touch your hair to know
What it is to be alive
And your golden strands
Would linger inside me all night
Until the morning when I awake to death
Are all angels as lonely as us?

The same faces are now leaving
And new voices are heard
Coming up the stairs
Past the bathroom
And there is a burst of cold air
From the front door that shuts quickly
With the wind
I opened my mouth to speak
And the voice of an old man
Came out to represent me
Me! the old man now at the counter
When did the tables turn this way?
I became suddenly older than the young man
That I was speaking to
He became my son and I his distant father

I speak no bitterness but only laugh at words
That shine like the sun off the snow
And pattern themselves against the sweater he wears
The sight of red and grey now forming
It's own voice in the air before me
And my angel passes by me and heads down the stairs
My voice has scared her away

She is speaking to her fiance
And I am jealous, loveless, and heartbroken
He speaks to her like most men would
And bores me more than words can describe
Oh, how ugly he makes her
She walks beside me and goes to the kitchen
He folds his newspaper and follows her
Dropping his coffee cup in the bus bin
As if he owns the place
There are a few words exchanged between him and the chef
And he says goodbye and walks out the door
And my angel resumes her beauty

Half of the cafe is empty now
And those who are left are quiet
And speak slowly
How they cherish each word

The old man and his Harper Lee character looks
Comes to the counter with coffee order
And surprises his lover with a cookie
That she would be expecting if she knew him
But all men claim to be romantic in that sense
And all men believe they are going the extra mile
Gregory Peck look-a-like you have fallen fifty yards behind
He walks out and his happy for the moment
Then Jimmy Stewart sits beside me at the counter
And appears angry when I start speaking to him
He is in financial despair

The crowd is now asleep
But for the man with the red beard
And his naive views on women
He is now sitting with his old man friend
And a lady in old blonde hair

Who appears from nowhere   .
I just can't remember her face

Middle aged man and wife
With young attractive brunette daughter
Are dressed as if New York has frozen over
They have walked from their house
On Coldwater Street
And are proud that they still look wonderful
The world stops for them as soon as the door opens
And I am not bitter over their beauty
My angel smiles at a remark
And I become bitter after that

More coffee and all returns to place
This is my last cup
Although I can't imagine what the bottom looks like
There are little puddles on the floor
All are clear and none are coffee
The nervous waiters spill coffee on their skin
Before the floor becomes soiled
Their own bodies become scarred before
The image of grace leaves the cafe
For once I am in the company of folks who care
Doesn't matter what for
Even if it is just for the immaculate face of their floor
Holy wetted virgin marble

This time when I stir my coffee
Looking out over the large dining area
I am drawn more to the empty spaces
Where the ghosts of diners still sit
And pay no attention in fact to the last three people
In the corner with their beautiful brunette daughter
Jimmy Stewart character still sits beside me
And looks at my wrists
One writing a poem and the other housing a bracelet
With silver band that shackles my thoughts
I've given up on his thoughts on me

The angel and her sweet European skin
Stretching out her arms like a dancer
I watch this single act of grace

From my side sight to the kitchen
She slips a piece of Swiss cheese between her lips
And will occasionally sip from her coffee mug
Which is identical to mine
But for the dribble marks from the hole in my lips
Your sad eyes and silent mouth
Have pierced pieces of me that I never knew I had

And suddenly the cafe is again busy
I am at the counter with Jimmy Stewart
Who is on the phone with his wife
Who doesn't really care all that much
About his plans for the day

Sweet angel, my goddess
I will speak to you in a dream of Sundays

A House in New Marlborough-

There is a room of snow in New Marlborough
There are four crooked frames in a corner
A painting on a chair by the door
A coat rack where broken hearts hang
And a couch with seamless quilts

There is a cat that sleeps in the bedroom
Where the echoes of children wander
There are voiceless women
And shelves of loveless men
In the walls there are cries of wind

In the halls there are shadows of morning
And windows silenced in sunlight
There are wells of summer grass
There are whispers of salt water kisses
And a stillborn lullaby in the cradle

In New Marlborough there are young photographs
There are girls in red scarves
There are sisters in glass coral frames
And mothers in the glow of candle wax
Beside bed frames there are tired sandals

There are fingertips worn on the windows
There are cloaks of full moon curtains
And sleepless nights in broken footprints
There are bottles of moonlight and flowers
There are quiet eyes in December

Your Voice-

At this time, who watches?
The radio's playing, but who listens?
Be glad and sing instead
Listen to your voice
For your voice is beauty
Even to the ears of the deaf
To the minds of many
Your voice remains silent
Who will love your voice?
If you do not love your voice
You will become deaf
To all the other sounds of life

------Snow Poems------

Snow #1-

Remembering the snow
And wet mountain tops
I sat in white
Dressed dark
Before the day's end

Snow #2-

Saw that snow fall
Inch an hour over the roads
Over the thin white line
From home to the fields

It blanketed the path
You walked from the car
To the doorstep

It made clear the definition
Between the sky and the trees
When all went dark
And the rains came

By then you were inside
Beside my still body
Quiet as death

Snow #3-

Was on a winter's night
I took myself inside the house
To hide a while from the cold
And wait out the dark in solitude

She stepped in soft
From a wander in the snow
And as her boots came up the wooden steps
I thought of winters long before

For nights on end I bid her stay
Until I could not let her go

Snow #4-

And stepping out the door
Rounding the house on the path
I came across a winter's night
Silent and still, waiting for nothing

The windows shone red and green
And golden glows of a child at rest

I stepped into the moonlight
And caught a breath of cold air
Fresh as new birth
Yet tainted as first sin

Snow #5-

We lay the bottle down
Beside the bed as I awoke
And I stepped from the door to the snow

Quitting the night for the morning
Quitting the warm for the dark

Across the street and into the white

Who would have thought that we'd still
Awake each day anew

Snow #6-

Wind came in cold through
Each crack in the window
Until we buried ourselves
Not in snow, but in blankets

Sheltered yet exposed
Covering up the glasses
And drawing the shades

We couldn't wait for morning
To reveal the damage we'd done

Snow #7-

Stepped into a snowdrift
Lasting the length of our street

There, stationary, watching,
I saw the river in pieces
Of ice breaking apart
For separate shores

I thought of you there in the window
Watching me

Snow #8-

In through the window
That blessed light
Quickly turning to a
Pale shade of white

She rolled over as
I turned from the bed
To gaze out at the
New morning as it fell
Flake by flake to the ground

Snow #9-

She stays beside me
But when she's gone
She's simply not there anymore

Lost among the winter
Sometimes I'll see her
From the window
Walking blind in the night

Snow #10-

The sun always returns
To this half of the world
That is a fact

No matter the snow
And the cold of dead winter
The sun always returns

Entering into the days
The light lasts longer
Than any darkness
Until next year

Snow #11-

The smell still fresh
On my hands
What a way to end the day

I wipe the snow from my shoulders
And stomp off the cold from my boots
Moving my way up the stairs
Or back into the night

Snow #12-

Home in the dark
Nothing but a belief

And morning comes
We both know this

Stockings hung and heater lit
Tree's beside the window
Dry as ashes

You take your stance
And all that's left
Is bed clothes shed
And an empty longing

Snow #13-

Sixty degrees at midnight
A cigarette in your hand
Walking willingly along the ice path
Holding the flame as a parasol

As the rain drops fall
One to the other winking
I await the silent vibrations
Of your feet on the stairs

Snow #14-

Saw in the sky
The first sign of spring
On a warm December night

You were there
Six feet under the rain
Rushing by at riverside

When the snow comes
I know that our beliefs
Coincide one to the other
With nothing on the earth

You and I are different
And that's all we know

Snow #15-

Temperature broke and lowered
Suddenly we were outside
And twenty-four degrees at noon

You wore my jacket
And I took the steps too far
Starting the car for the day

Now home after the drive
And remembering the snow that fell
Over the headlights

I wonder if outside the dark window
A blanket of white is coating
The place where we now live
And if you stay safe
Where you are tonight

Snow #16-

All the white mornings
By the window I recall
Her face set as slate

I should have stayed

We always said that night
Was fine for us back then

Ten years after the fact
Will we look back
On all the winter nights
Spent alone?

Snow #17-

All the while spent alone
You and I had it right
All those years ago

Now within the days passing
And the spring coming
I question what it was
That really kept us apart

And I know it was us

End of a Warm February Day-

A warm February day and she's changing into a dress
as I'm sitting at the table guessing where the arrow
is landing on the thermometer just outside the window
beside the couch where the cat is asleep

She doesn't love me but what does it matter?
The air is warm and I'm without a coat
walking through town beside her
She's got a design on her tights
that has the look of pine needles
lining the floor of an old-wood forest

When we get to the restaurant everyone stares
When we sit down the people go back
to eating their overpriced meals
with small side dishes of parsley
and chicken liver pate

She wants a smile that shows no emotion;
that shows nothing but joy,
but there is nothing in here of joy
You want love? Maybe I can give it to you
Just don't leave me tonight

The waitress leaves and doesn't come back
when the meal is over and we try to catch
her sad Spanish eyes, dark as mine but empty
When we get the check, we slip in the money
and go out the door as soon as she brings back
the credit card with a cheap pen
but no mint...

Burgundy doesn't do good on my age
She sees that look in my eyes and when
I put my arm around her as we walk into
the night, she kisses me like she's sorry
Where did you go? she's asking

and maybe I'm answering in my own way

We do a u-turn in her driveway when she
changes her mind about me coming over
and soon I'm beside my car and she's telling
me that she's got to leave
She says it's okay, and that I don't need to go there,
to that dark place that I love
I know that... I kiss her and she drives away...

There's a pan of old coffee on the stove
and a used Japanese mug on the counter
And I've been sitting here for hours
just trying to get sober again
and maybe I'm just paranoid and need sleep
All I know is she says that she will see me tomorrow
and I will wait half the morning for the call
Tonight I fear sleep more than sobriety

Love-

When my world was ideal
I caught for you a dove
I became a prisoner
Sentenced to death by love
You were then my queen
And I your humble slave
I caught for you a dove
And let it fly away

Love Thus Far-

Never deny your woman all the love you have, especially if it is for her.

Never deny yourself the acceptance of love, because it may not be there when you wake up beside a stranger.

Be Jesus to a Lazarus and judge what is worse: life or death; love or longing.

The ways of love are many.

Do not deny yourself of the roads that bypass each other for the sake of the road you're on.

In the course of each new love, a lifetime will pass before your eyes.

Clouds-

Cold in the wisps of wind
that take the place of the sun
that no longer shines for winter
but harbors feelings for summer
like a dying man holds
the longing for life

Where are the thoughts
that once held the hands
of small children
taking first steps
out of their home
to see the sky above them
glow with radiance
at the crack of noon
when the clouds lift above the earth?

Who houses the impact of the eyes
that lift the clouds from the bay
and proclaim light to each other
the only way they know how?

Cafe at Dusk-

Empty tables now line the walls
of a room once full with people,
both young and old, just hours ago

How dark the streets become
once the shops close for the night
and turn their lights dim
until all that there is to light the way
is the glow of the sliver of moon
that has caught to an old fragment
at the corner of Railroad street

The cafe that housed conversations
just a short time ago
is now lifeless and cold
but for a few crumbs, reminiscent of
the laughter of two men
catching up on the last decade
over muffins and coffee
They parted when the darkness crept
over the small town and beckoned
them home to their wives and
children in the suburbs,
only twenty minutes from each other

The town became dark
and not even lit with the
Christmas lights, left over for months
in the shop windows

Empty tables now line the walls
of a small cafe on Main street
where hours ago, the young and old
were embraced by conversation

Darkness-

I wear them,
the ribbons,
that you tied
on my wrists
to tether me
to the earth
that you tied
around yours

you told me
the earth's
greatest charm
is keeping us
grounded,
when we
try to escape

before you
found Virgo
and loosed
Orion's belt
I watched you
slip into a
piece of darkness
that I once
held for you
to sleep in

Halves-

Our broken bodies torn and bent in halves
Pasted together again like popsicle stick dolls

We found our worst halves across the world
With hidden wings and covered memories

We began with nothing and ended with less
At the shore that swallowed the earth

In flames we heard the cry of fallen angels
Skinless and blinded as we are this evening

Now we are ashamed of the soulless bodies
That we never chose to wear

Surreal-

You said the word was "surreal"
That was the word that was your life
You said that each moment spent
Was a surreal moment
In which any second you would awake
And find yourself back in yesterday's life
But it was never that way
You never woke from your life
To find that he was just a lie
Or that you were just an actor
No, you were both subject to the truth
In which you both set the scene
And you both delivered your parts
In the only way you could
Honest, humble, and surreally transparent

Avocado-

I ran into you at the store
in the shortest check out line,
with an avocado and deodorant in hand–
or was that me in your fingers,
held tight like the last avocado on earth?

The cashier did his part
by not smiling or acknowledging us,
only sliding the items over his scanner

All was paid for in full
by a credit card with a name
that once resembled yours

I lost you to the parking lot
where an old friend caught your attention
as I started the car and slowly drove on,
leaving you with the avocado
that I saw in your hand
as I stopped for a man at the crosswalk

Despite the darkness and flash of headlights
I still made out your small figure
and the harsh outline of your nose,
standing beside the store with a guilty look
plastered all over your thighs

The Gates-

The gates of her bedroom
are guarded by thin air
There are thorns of roses
on the path to her bed
Black dresses line the
wooden floorboards
When night falls there
are shadows of the men
who fell into her darkness

Insane Old Man-

The insanity has come to the coffee shop
With the slow moving and the rustles
Pressing the money counter and the scone lender
Dropping the quarters to the cup outside the door
Where the blue eyes wait in Sunday sunshine
And the old man shakes early before my table
Leaving me the questions of sane and sanity meanings
And wondering what they mean to the sandwich on his plate
Or if it matters from this cafe seat distance
His voice is mine and shakes like mine
Speaking to no one and eventually the cook
Who brings out the crepes and the world rejoices
To the sound of the horn over the speakers
God, don't let me be this old man

The Perfect Match-

Naked off and on-
a perfect match.
She was changing
as I was changing,
hoping for the best.

We became ready
to shed our bodies
and lie beneath each other
having changed ourselves
and lost all desire

Now on the coat rack
are the thin sheets of skin
that once clothed and
encompassed our
pale and faded faith

Friday Morning Poem-

Once again staring into black
and brown swirled coffee
in a white lip smeared cup
at a stainless steel counter top
thinking of a woman

Flower-

There's a flower withering
on the bathroom sink,
reaching for water
but unable to find any
People come and go
They wash their hands
They brush their teeth
They shut off the faucet
and leave the flower with nothing
Unable to move,
the flower has no choice
but to pray that the
right person comes along

Oil on Water-

my hand running
down your thigh
the feel of skin
the sound of flesh
on flesh

of wet on dry

of oil on water

you took everything

The Dance-

Love is the shapeless dance
that shines in the light
of young women
When the eyes are dyed blue
and the last man has left
the dance and the dancer remain
thick as cancer in the bone
Long after the dancer has died
the dance waltzes on

Abandoned-

There's a list of those who loved me
There's a list of those who left
There is a picture of a woman
There are many pictures of my friends
There are lies to tell my family
dated back to who knows when
There is the lonely abandoned feeling
resting somewhere beneath your bed

Blind-

I woke from my sleep
and found her arm
wrapping itself around me
as if she were drowning and I was
the only drift wood left
I found the darkness unbroken
in the sky outside her window
We fell asleep beside each other
not needing to make love
knowing how our bodies felt
my chest against her back
And then it was morning
and I fell back asleep in her arms
so as to dream a little longer

Thinking About It Again-

The house would be quiet at times
when the wind was not blowing
and the pipes were not aching for warmth
She would move slowly over the wood floor
and move slower over the mattress
that would slide slowly into the wall,
rattling the shade on the lamp
All the while the boys slept
like the angels that we once were

Keeping the Secret-

A rose hip body
kept me quiet
The children slept
beside our bedroom
We broke the silence
with our laughter
As the children slept
and dawn drew upon us

Past Sketch of Cafe-

I step into a small cafe at closing time
and order a coffee to go
but sit anyways at a small table
between two older couples
who have nothing to say
but still find something every few minutes

One lady says to her husband
that he should write a memoir
and I know that he knows he should
but still falls asleep every night
not being able to get it down
and plus he's too old for sex
so he doesn't have much going for him
and should probably die
no offense

The other couple, the one behind me,
speaks loudly but I'm too stuck on my book
to really care and besides the other old lady
keeps staring me down like I'm road kill
on the side of a highway and she's
an old vulture with nothing better to do
but remember the old days and pick apart
the ones that are yet to come
she was a fox in her day

I get a call on the phone, look at it,
and put it back in my pocket for a rainy day
hoping for a message and not getting one
but what does it matter, she's a whore
and I've got nothing to say to her

I feel like the old man, thinking back on it
I feel very much like the old man
who sits before me at this cafe today
as I duck out of the cold and try to kill
some time and some memories with one throw

of that old Jesus metaphorical stone of mine,
which is essentially caffeine

He doesn't get around much,
just teaches his class at the college
and watches the kids fall in love,
get pregnant, and die of overdoses
sometimes purposely and other times
for one reason or another accidentally,
but at least there was a reason

I could stare into his eyes, if he let me
but he's been watching his wife
who has been watching her coffee
and not really thinking of anything to say
but either way they have enough entertainment
just looking out the window and gawking

I have the collection of poetry, unedited,
on the table before me and they see it
and wonder what it is and I do too
I flip through it every now and then
and nod slowly as if to signify that I am working,
which I guess I am in one way or another

I put on my coat to leave and almost knock a man
off of his seat with the swing of my arm
not noticing how small the cafe really is,
but feeling the eyes of the school teacher's wife
on me still as if I've got the scarlet letter,
which has recently been postmarked
but hasn't arrived at my house yet

As I walk out the door and back down Lark street
I watch the two old folks donning their own coats
and rising to return back to their lives
though both glad to have slipped away for a moment
and taken shelter in that small cafe
where we all left a few of those dirty little memories

The Story and the Trade-

The sun going down,
not by it's own doing,
but of mine,
walking toward it
and pushing it
to the treetops

The story of winter
coming into spring
on a walk through
the valley of midday
with no questions
of the end of the week

The trade of my fingers
typing to the bone
for the perfect word
or the perfect phrase;
the one that will cause you
to cry for me again

The story and the trade of poetry,
 whatever that may be,
and whatever I choose it to be,
remembering the silhouette
of the trees with the fire
dying behind them

Tonight there is only one trick
and I call it the lie

Being Sober-

I gave up drinking
last Friday night
and now sit in the
chair, arms crossed,
eyeing the bottle of wine
that I've kept sitting
on my floor for
a cold night like this
She's a fine bottle

When I call her
she answers me
like a dog
that won't shut up
I relieve her
and she cools me down
and when she's down
I've got that dirty feeling
that she's done me wrong

Soon her black dress
is halfway beneath the bed
and I know she's here
if not in the dress
so I search the house
in a frantic state
until I awake in the morning
in disgust of the bottle,
empty on the floor

A Blonde This Time-

It all became very loud
and I knew that I had to leave
but she was there and
walking slowly toward me
giving me the look that
I was just beginning to
get used to

She was young and naive
just as I remembered her
but her body felt worn
as I leaned for the embrace
that ended the evening

I said goodnight and
walked out the door
and suddenly it was morning
and I was here again

I took off my jacket
and ordered myself a coffee
trying hard not to think of her

Love Letter-

There are many questions
I ask each day of my life
but I never question
if you loved me

Even after all these years
I search for this love
that I let slip away
without a fight

For all the years apart
that are still to come,
know that I miss you
everyday

Living with the Mistake-

The hair on my head has wilted
and the skin on my hands is torn
like the arms and legs of the woman
that I've got stuffed inside my mind
who smiles when I close my eyes

I could have become anything
but became a roadmap to nowhere
and a cut up poem of a girl
pasted to the eyes behind my mind
where I rock her endlessly to sleep

I grant myself the serenity tonight
and share the same reflection of the
black silhouettes outside the window
beside the bed where I've chained
all of my fragmented nights

Prayer of Self-

Forgive me Lord
For I am sin
I'm the lonely man
That love let in

I am the father,
The misplaced son,
The sky above us,
The forsaken one

So Lord be willing
To help me sleep
And count me among
Your slaughtered sheep

The Siren-

My siren calls to me
nights on end with the voice
of the sea at my ear
and the dew of longing
on my lips

Where did she go
that took me so far
away from myself
and which of us
was it that left?

Who wipes dry
the tears at the siren's
cheeks, wet with laughter?

The night comes
to welcome home the vagrant,
the Godless being
of a man on the sea

When will the waters
surrender her secrets
and how many men
will resurface when they
are revealed?

Tonight I fear
that even God drowns

The Eternal Loss-

There was a time between the summer
and it's fall that we walked in the park
and held hands on the stone pathway
that led between the flower gardens
as the cool of the approaching autumn
chilled our arms.

all was fine. you wore a sweater and I
a shirt that I can't remember.

I took the sun from the sky that day
and saved it for the darkness
that I knew would eventually creep
back into your eyes where it belonged
somewhere between heaven
and my love for you.

in those days I counted myself lucky
for the love that you gave to me in the night
when I was beside myself in terror
and suckled anything that gave resemblance
to the light that I remembered.

in those days I could still remember the sun
and each time your cheeks flushed
in that cold September
I could still see what summer had left.

if I did any wrong to you in those hours,
know that it was the doing of someone
less than me.

I remember a fountain that day in the park
but I can't remember if the water ever flowed out
on those cold mornings.

somedays I still walk through the park
and look for you in the lilies,
realizing that winter has come.

The Sin Repeated-

The sin repeated day after day
continues to be repeated in my sleep.

I wake and can see the relics
of the last night scattered on the floor
under a thick layer of regret.

If it had to do with you;
if it had your smell;
even then I would regret.

Down below the bed I sometimes sweep up
ashes that bear your birthmarks and I swear
your freckles are within them.

I'll carry this body as my cross,
over my shoulder throughout the day.

I'll carry my soul like a memory
of someone that I used to know.

Somewhere beneath me is you,
like a grain of sand under my feet.

My day is a regret of past night times
spent sifting through the dust bowl for you.

Snow Walk-

The sun behind
a grey and white
clouded sky
with snowflakes
large and drifting
in a futile dance
to the river

All will be forgotten
someday

Who will hold
this memory
when we have
forgotten?

On the banks
of the river
nothing remains
but the linger
of a voice
that can't
be placed

Like the sense
of sight
this memory
will hold true
only as long
as we are
here

Testament-

From my corner I am
the quiet observer,
the documenter of all activities
under heaven.
This in my hand is the
testament of the lonely.
This is the overcoat thrown
over a flannel shirt
torn at the arms.
I am the observer of sunlight
pouring through the windows
at the other end of the room.
From my corner I have seen
the many things that I cannot forget.
I can see the world that sees me
and the world that cannot.
From my corner I am
the quiet observer
watching the young girl long
for the love of another woman.
From the corner I bless the
lesbians of this small town.
I bless the friend of a friend
and the father of that friend
just coming into sight.
I bless and document the world
who cares and the world
who does not
and I hold the testament of both these worlds.

The World Turns They Tell Me-

The world turns they tell me
Though I stay stuck in the night
Leaning over a darkened desk
Putting down the bottle

The world turns they tell me
As perpetual night stains the room
I'm putting down the bottle
As the morning begins to rise

The world turns they tell me
I'm never going there again
To the bottle, my compass
And to the darkness, my comrade

Monotone World Celebrations-

The world hears me now
as the voice from a drunken window
crying the last words
of a dying America

It is the cry from a window
high above a city sitting in ruin
waiting for a bill to be passed

A city that watches with wide eyes
as the world around it burns

That sits on doorsteps
with nothing but a two dollar beer
and a toy poodle

That cries nothing but lies
to the children in the pantry

This is the cry of a young man
who has seen what the world will do
to the children when they are released

This is the cry of a man
who gazes down at the dark figures
lining the pavement from north and south
to the end of the line
that is nowhere

This is the sigh of the couple
turning the corner in the rain

This is the wailing of the angels
that die in the darkness
of the rooftops that I see
through the steam outside my window

This is the cry of the angels

who sit drunk in the bars
only to awaken as pretentious
hipsters in coffee shops

This is the sound of the world
burning itself to the ground

This is the voice of your son
speaking to you from the face
of the sky

This is the son
who left you as a child and
crawled back only to find
it was too late

This is the son
who haunts you like the memory
of the father drinking himself
to the alleys where he cried night
and day for his safe release
from the jails of your mind

This is the son who cries
into the mouth of an empty bottle
that lies in perpetual spin
on the floors of youth

This is the son who drowned
at age seven and through
the grace of God was reincarnated
as a slave to Satan
the female deity

This is the son who fears nothing
but the rasp of a mother's voice

This is the cry of a son
who sits alone among the multitudes
who sit with black eyes and lipstick
smeared faces

This is the cry of a drunken stranger

who was once your son
but is now an old man at a desk
crying himself to sleep

This is the cry of the end of the world
which is only a scribble
on a short piece of paper

This is the son of the world
that did come to an end
as you sat and watched television

This is the son who began
his fifth round, sobered up,
and drove all the dents and dings home

This is the cry of your son
who tonight at his window
imagines the pavement is the
sweet rain of the Pacific

This is the cry that dies in silence

Revelation on Hill-

Today amid the dried thorns
that lay in the fading sunlight
I became not only someone else
but everyone else all at once

For a moment I became man
and I became the women too
The birds above my head,
yes, they were me and I them

The trees swayed to my mood
The sun rose and fell with me
The water wept away the sand
with the falling of my tears

For that given moment
the world and I were coexistent
and one in body
balancing the eternal scales

When I returned home to tell the news
I found nobody willing to listen
and thus locked myself in the bedroom
becoming a separate entity; therefore nothing

Two Young Lovers-

Two young lovers
Of white on white
Sit alone together
With ripped shirts
And torn knees
They speak the unspoken
And silence the spoken
And then there is only silence
How beautiful to love
And useless all the same
Two lovers, young and stupid
As the rest of us
Just a bit more naive
And it's all for the better
Life is too short for anything else

Words to the Colonel-

Tonight I will hide the moon
For she reminds me of you

Her sadness whispers softly
A name that I once knew

The glass is always full
For even emptiness is dense

One of us must lose in love
And we both know that it's not you

Another Regret-

The world could
have ended
for everyone
in the same
way it ended
for me
when I
saw you today
Now in the
darkness
I picture
all the things
I would change
as they hide
behind that
pretty face of yours

Sunday Morning Note to Baker-

Behind the counter
and through the window
where the secrets are kept,
a baker in the midst of morning
ties knots in plastic bags
and empties flour into tubs

She is alone for a time
before the staff arrives
and the customers follow

I am one of the customers
and I would follow her
into the outside world
if my coffee were not full
and keeping me tied here

She will say hello to me
when she steps to the counter
as she readies to leave

We know one another
but have not loved
and have never had enough reason
to become friends

This is a lonely note
to the girl in the kitchen
who keeps my mind occupied
on Sunday mornings

Bar Top-

The dark wood
Turned light by time
Like daylight to the drunk
Stepping out of the house
Realizing the world is still
Spinning

Glasses of ice water
Leaving rings on the counter

Limes on the bar top
In ceramic plates
Beside tumblers

Water glasses

Used whiskey

Dashed everything

Glass of water
At the end of a
Somewhat empty notebook

Still and unmoving
As the candlelight
I sit in the crowd–
The one that makes
All the noise

Many Nights Were Spent Alone-

During the night
I awoke in your house
where I knew I would have to return

I searched for you
but I found the darkness first

It was myself and the cold wind of winter
outside the windows where no light shone

Many nights were spent alone
in this house

Many chimes rang out
for no one to hear

Listen now and you will still hear the sound
of my breath
running through your split ends

Listen now and you will still hear the sound
of a door bolted from the outside
trying to be opened

Listen now and you will hear the sound
of my precious savior's laughter from the porch
where she holds the key

In the darkness I waited for you
knowing that around one of the corners
you were standing there
waiting to pull the knife on me

Forsythia-

You trim the forsythias
on the kitchen table
with the rusty clippers
from the garage.
You give the flowers
the illusion of life.
You ready the vase.
You cut the branches to twigs
and the petals fall
from the table to the floor,
where they are forgotten.
When we grow old,
trim me gently
as you would the forsythias,
letting me slip slowly
back into the blossom
of the springtime.

Shadow in a Field-

Each morning I pass a field
of blossoming bushes
in the seven o' clock sunlight.
I swear that your hair
is in the forsythias
and your feet in the hyacinths,
but even you, my love,
are too dark to see.
I know that in time,
these mornings will fade
and I will be left
with the dried stems
of the flowers
that line my dash board.
These thoughts do not keep
me from searching for you
in the yellows and blues.
What thoughts arise in your mind
to keep you from revealing
your body in the field?
What visions keep you painted
to your stick figure shadow?
I pass the field in the evening
and watch the gold turn to copper
when the sun slips
behind the last mountain top.
When the day is done,
I pray silently for the lonely place
that I imagine your shadow will sleep.

Paul Sleeping-

In and out slowly
The breathing of a child
Asleep on the couch
His blond hair falling
On his flushed face
And a speck of red lint
On the tip of his nose
His t-shirt inside out
His tranquility mastered
At the age of four
The peaceful afternoon nap
That the cat cannot disturb
I do not wake him
I only observe his youth
And feel my own
Slipping further away
With each breath
Slowly, in and out

Birches-

Hung between branches
I am surrounded
Birch littered bones
Line the forest
They rest day and night
With or without me
And I will rest assured
Knowing they also rest
When the forest is still
No words need to be spoken
But does the world need me
In order to be still?
I know the birches rest here
While I rest in bed
I am surrounded now
Hung between branches
And littered birch bones

Murky Window-

I see her through the window
I am once again gazing past
My own reflection in the murky glass
Looking beyond myself to find her,
Dark and blurred by the wall between us
Silent and empty by the distance
Worthwhile and desired by our absence
If she sees me, I cannot tell
Her figure fades away from the window
And I walk to my car
In the midst of a pear blossom snow squall

Inside-

Inside I know that outside
is brighter than this desk light
The sun needs no outlet
to let you know that you're alive

Before the Rain-

Before the rain you told me
That the stars held a place for us
And that all good thoughts
Eventually resurfaced within the darkness
And that with enough of these thoughts
We could secede from the earth
And climb the war field into the heavens
–We ourselves the shooting stars from the sky
As if from a musket

When I look into the clouds
I like to imagine that the grey
Is the smoke of many lovers
At last leaving the grasp of earth

Untitled-

In few words
Speak love to me

Dreamer-

If I wake beside you in the night
And you are awake also
Press my head back to the pillow
Otherwise I may leave
And never come back

Apartment Poem-

What lines have crossed my eyes today?
When the sun comes through
the bathroom window, I sometimes feel
that it is all new again.
When I take the towel and dry myself
and walk slowly through the hallway
and the photos in the dark,
I question the strength of the one
who carries the sun beneath his arm,
but not the insecurity that allows
him to hide it beneath the moon.

When you leave me,
your sepia figure between the door frame,
know that within my stone body
a hand reaches
to grace the hem of your skirt.

So Thank Them, God-

Who do I thank for those
little moments?

The times that the sunlight shone upon you,
bright with no regret,

The afternoons on Market street

The tents and stalks
of sugar cane

These days I find your red shirt in the strawberries
while shopping at the store
and the liquid curves of your body
tight against the outline of the world
within your picture frame on the desk

My mind replays the sway of your skirt
when your figure leaves my door
and but for your absence
all is much the same
she even looks like you sometimes

Somedays I see myself in solitude
forever and
I know to thank you for that

Why I Write Poetry-

Each poem is a question. I do not make statements, but ask permission. I ask whether you agree that the fields are green or if the birds make sound when they lift off the telephone wire. I ask you if the sun rises from North to South or up to down. I ask who you are and who God is and if I am indeed His face and hands; if I am the image of my own immortal longing. I ask you why the flowers are in love with the riverside and why the hyacinth has withered early. I ask you in colors and apostrophes; in shades and semicolons; in lines and rambles; in peace and the utter quiet of midnight from my couch in the valley. You can hear me through my thoughts and I can hear my questions in the air, mingling and waltzing with the answers above the vines of summer squash and zucchini and the rows of carrot stalks sprouting from the earth. I ask you to drive me home in the night when my memory of home has failed me. I ask you where the fields have gone when I am writing on the sidewalk. I ask you for the smell of the Siberian iris in its fairy ring around the garden gnome. I ask for a reminder and I get the silent voice of God from my pen.

Extent of Knowledge-

The world is paved
but not in gold.
Someone once told me
that heaven is much
the same.

Nobody knows what comes next.
That is what can be said
of the extent of knowledge
entrusted upon us.

A weed between the cracks
doesn't signify hope, but
futile persistence of a
species against something too large.

Someday we all fail.
That is all we know.

Remembering-

This is what they say
you'll remember
at the moment
when the rope slips
or when the match falls
or when the hope comes
and you can't quite catch it
in time.

This is the smile of
your mother in the sand
or your father's mustache,
wet, as he takes you
out past the buoys.
This is what they say
you'll remember.

This is the flatbed
going sixty-five down 7.
The street bench at midnight.
The empty moonlit bottle
from Spain,
sitting trackside on Silver street.

Who do we bury there
among the leaves?
My shoes are too torn
for these questions.
My mind is too closed
for outsides.

Dry grass between
the thyme.
Green river stones
beneath the water.
Dark brown eyes
in the rearview.

These are the sights
they say will
stare you down
in those last moments.
These are the eyes of the child
staring through the paternal body
in the mirror.

This is what they say
you'll remember.
The taste of the alloy kiss
just before you tell yourself
it's alright.

Summertime, Harlemville-

The fan in the window
blows heat on heat.
The summer is dry.
The dirt is cracked.
The fields are brown.
The pond has a shy swimmer
on it's dock
who seeks water.

I'll sit in the apartment,
look out the window
and see sweat drenched soldiers
of the marketplace
trudging in packs of fives
and sevens.
Children and adults.
A baby in the arms
of the mother,
both in tears.
There is an iced coffee
indoors.

Early morning the farmers
– mostly women –
go out to the fields
and harvest crops
in beige shorts
and rolled sleeve t-shirts.

At night we die in the heat
and think about life
as we stare into the moon
rising above the houses
on the hill.

Dust-

Dust gathers
on the floorboards
beneath the bookshelf.
Once, in another building,
the same dust gathered,
coating the floor
that propped up all
those empty pages.
What are we
writing that keeps
us all so
intrigued?
The dust is
gathering around us.
In the old room
I held negatives
across the light
and watched the characters
bleed as they melted
in the flame.
Dust was on the
candle.
In the small
places such as this,
it is an honor
to be forgotten
by time
and left alone to settle
across the floorboards.

Heartbreak-

A heart like anyone's
I take her hand
I make her unique
To her life I bring meaning
To her eyes I take away
the look of naivete
and simplicity that one
carries when they are
expecting something beautiful

Flower Petals-

They say that like a flower
all life blooms and withers

I hear the telephone ring
and I know it is a call
but not the call

All telephones ring the same message
in different chimes
in different time

And the church bell tolls
for the dead
and those refusing to die

They say that all will fall
like the petals from a soda glass vase

The wind will interrupt
the undisturbed process of being
and pinpoint each touch of
the willow on the skin

That is what they say

Rain Poem-

It's not the room
That holds me here
To the spot in the valley
Wide Open
Exposed to the elements
What elements?
This room is my house

I know that like my sister
I am alive in the rain
I am drinking a cup of tea
Daily in the rain
Sober or not
I watch the rain
Drip from the gutter
That ever present reminder

Ever present

I am alive
This is my house
In this valley
I've made my home

I watch the rain
Trickle from home
To the outer facets of life

Driving-

There's a song on the radio
and I'm driving with the
windows fogging up as a
storm pours down on me
thinking how I miss my baby and
thinking I could miss my life
if I were to guide myself to
the rail, dying
a tragic death

You know, when I pass those
little crosses on the side of the
road, I think how embarrassing
it is to die

Playback-

Thin and recognizably plain
Ourselves in someway or another
Watching a playback of our life
Coming in and out of coffee shops
Just as we come in and out of love affairs
Just as we come in and out of the divine light
Just as a new born baby comes into life crying
We grasp at the unobtainable
We grasp at the indecipherable
We grasp at whatever holds true
We play the croquet of the fallen angels
We trace our silhouette on the projector's bed sheet
And each day replay for the sake of memory

Cigarettes-

Darkened night of clouds
White and black in the air
Between the stars
and she's on the steps
with a cigarette ember
lighting the ring
around her mouth

If she thinks of me
I wonder what she thinks
of me

Up the stairs
I've got the tired face
of a man remembering

Midnight Drive-

I hear her calling
Through the pines
I hear her calling
In the night
The naked moonlight
Echoes her calling
And the highway
                    runs wild

Pocket Stone-

Flowers on the sink side

Dry and withered kitchen life

Cats eyes and reminiscent scents

Oh, love changer

Card holder of the tables

The tables of changing lives

The sound of feet on stairs

And the feel of numbing sands

You bring the wind's change
And the season's change
And the autumnal cleansing
To the open windowed home

River Words-

She lights a cigarette in dark
and I'm able to trace her face
by the way the orange paints her bright

She takes the pages from her bag
and writes a letter to God
or just herself,
letting it float in the river

I write my words and she takes it
into the water

What was it that I wrote?

I sat to think as we watched the paper pass
beneath the log that crossed to the other side

When she stood to leave,
I felt the same lost feeling
and the loss of something more

Portland Blues #4-

dusk in last October day
a new week turning
turning a new month
falling to another

this is what they tell us about:
how time passes unnoticed
and how one day
we're too late

some nights she won't see me
she won't look at me
it's October 31st
and I'm coming down

dusk in late October
an old day starting over again

I've been here before, but when?
don't tell me I'm here again

it's nine PM and I'm coming down

when the rain falls as it did tonight,
I remember the previous years
on stone streets
I remember other years
and faces speaking silent words

you were there among them
I know this
arching the crook of your legs
over the city

Gaylord's-

on fog rising cool mornings
I could take the sidewalk
and leave the girl in sheets
to have a dance among the faces
there within the confines
of the shadows we've painted

I still remember the faces
one to the other staring
voiceless lips speaking
simple words that I myself
took for truth

Snow-

now remembering the snow
and white mountain tops

I sat in white
dressed dark
before the day's end

and saw that snow fall
inch by hour over the roads
and over the thin white line
from home to fields

blanketing the path
I watched you walk from the car
to the doorstep

making clear the definition
between the sky and the trees

and before the rain
you were safe beside my body
quiet as death

-

inside myself the solitude
taken from a winter's night
and clouded over in disillusion

where so many nights I asked to stay
until you could not let me go

where I came to you
a golden glow of a child at rest

where I stepped into the moonlight
and caught a breath of cold air

fresh as new birth
yet tainted as first sin

-

and I am awake in the night
beside the bed

quitting the night for the morning
and the warmth for the dark
still believing that we awaken
each day anew

-

the wind coming
through each crack in the windows
keeping us buried in the bed
waiting for morning to reveal
the damage we'd done

-

stepped into a snowdrift
lasting the length of our street
and there, stationary, watching,
I saw the river in pieces
of ice breaking apart
for separate shores

there in the cold
I thought of you
in the window
watching me

-

you rolled over
to gaze out at the
new morning as it fell
flake by flake to the ground

-

you stay beside me
but when you're gone
you're gone

simply not there anymore

-

lost among the winter
sometimes I'll see her
from the window
walking blind in the night

-

the snow still fresh on my hands
what a way to end the day

-

home in the dark
nothing but a belief

and morning comes
we both know this

-

Quickly-

"Quickly," she said,
"before we even know
                     we're gone."

7X7 Box-

Four sides symmetrical
Stained by the carpenters thumb
Sanded smooth as skin in summer
Pine or balsa, timber framed
or held by steel

      The world is a square
made up of 1X6 boards
cut down to a small box
resting at my feet

What are the walls
      that we build?
Who are we keeping
      in the cold?
Which side of ourselves
do we not want to see
      in the night?

When you rise from the floor
kissing each part of my legs
I imagine the walls of your being
rising above my head
and I can't tell if I
am within your 7X7 box
or on the outside
trying to get in

Assessment-

This is the room where I keep my thoughts

Eight feet below the ceiling are the chests
of the days that have gone by

Ex-girlfriends in the ratchet straps

Old friends in the suitcases

Past projects in the ziplock bags

This is the room where I have spent
all the days of my once upon a time future

These are the peach crates where I store
the pay stubs of childhood

These are the fed-ex boxes from the first
time I moved out of a woman's house

And this is the same chair I sat in
when I watched the last one leave

Not Knowing What to Do-

The street is prepared but nobody has noticed.
A woman crosses to the other side and
slips inside a door.

The sounds of Monday morning are heard
from the storefronts and from the cafe counters
and bookstore bathrooms.

She is there and I've stopped
drinking again.

She's there in the fabric of my clothes,
constricting me and keeping me whole.

A pain in my chest from Saturday keeps me
from lining up my possibilities for today,
still she is there in the idea of something better.

I've never been a big fan of dogs, but
they are here in the coffee shop as
another woman crosses to the other side,
this time with a child
and a husband
and another child.

When the parade begins it's hard to tell
the marching band from the radio song.
As the parade passes it's hard to tell
the veterans from the spectators,
the old men from the children on the sidewalk.

Some of us go outside for cigarettes and
some of us stay inside for the silence.

Before the band is passed, the music
is already over.

The radio speakers have begun again and
the simple sound of Monday morning returns.

And still, she is there in the stitches.

October Poem-

You and winter
Are similar to the night

I see you as if
From a crowded street
And you see me

But you turn to the crowd
And the crowd is everywhere

We pass without a word

Winter has a way of keeping
Strangers from wanting to meet
And people from touching each other

And loneliness manifests itself

The nights of autumn tumble
When the cold air comes

And I see you there
As if from a car window
On a crowded turnpike

We glance and see each other
Through the glass

A few lights flash
And we are past
Simply not there anymore

Winter has this way of winding
Time around its fingers

Words around my mind

Women around the soft thistle
Of days that pass

Leaving Home-

Something that could have been anything
Brought me from my home today

It could have been that sunlight
That has long since faded

It could have been that breeze
That long ago died down

Or it could have been winter,
That old friend I saw last night,
Peering 'round a corner on the
Cold walk from work

It could be anything today
That brought me from my home
And into the town

Something simple as the seasons
And dark as the turning of time

Something as fine as thread being sewn
Between the patchwork of days

Something as striking as the way a face looks
The moment it leaves your life
And is gone into infinity

Quick Cafe Mornings, Low Cafe Nights-

So many quick days spent
watching men and
watching women
    in dresses of winter
    and gowns of summer
and haunting memories
    of the other days that
        we know must come

And you are there
    as well as I am there
and we are here within
    the memory of each other
        watching each other
            on quick cafe mornings
                and low cafe nights

So many hours kept together
    both you and I
    the keepers of time
    on quick days of coffee
    and low nights of wine

You are there beside me
    making observations of time

    There within my thoughts
        your thoughts flow
            and what I observe
        of the thoughts are there
    in what is observed by many
–and the days are long
    but quick all the same

And many nights too
    are spent alone

                    within these confines
            of open mornings

Many nights are spent in
            time with the morning
and many nights in tune
            with the sun

These days are yours and,
            if on occasion only, mine

When the thoughts are gone from
            me, they come to you, but
            when they are gone from you
                    I only know that they
                            are gone from me forever

Still you hold the thoughts that
at once were held by me
and I am there in the
way that you are there and I
miss you all the same
            as I miss all the thoughts
                    I held,
            that you now hold

Nothing,
            nothing gets in the way
                    of the world
            and the world has
                    no cares
                            and I am here
            and you are here, but
                    the world notices
                            no one
                    –it just is

The world that I see knows
            no good or bad
            and knows no existence
or non-existence
            and I know that
it was never born

–it never sprung–
and therefore will never
die–it will never fall

I know that, like you,
I will fall and that,
like you, I was born
in summer

The world does not know us;
for there is nothing the world knows
and the world does not wish
to know us;
for longing
does not exist

–the world simply is

On quick cafe mornings,
who will know the way
that I feel in face
to face encounters with the
world that knows me
and the world that
does not?

You are the world that knows my
face and the world that holds
me still

You give me grace, you give
me pressure, you give me
the extraction of beauty
from yourself and of
my own existence

You exist, so I exist, and without
you there is no me and without
the way I feel, you feel
nothing

I coincide and coexist
and you are my shadow

and I am your stone pillar
    in the sun

    And what is it that
        shines on us in
            the night?

You are there in the confines
    of the morning
and stay with me in
    the darkness of the
        night, where even
            beneath the light of
                the stars, we are
                    in the eternal
                        darkness of
                            unity

                  Your world is my world
              and in my world
            I am in you and
        you are, in turn,
            me

        In the night you are
    there in the confines
        of the stars

And morning breaks and
    unity lingers

        And the world
            simply is

Made in the USA
Charleston, SC
09 December 2015